POP STANDARDS
FOR EASY CLASSICAL PIANO
15 OF THE BEST ARRANGED BY PHILLIP KEVEREN

— PIANO LEVEL —
INTERMEDIATE

ISBN 978-1-4950-9414-9

HAL•LEONARD®

7777 W. BLUEMOUND RD. P.O. BOX 13819 MILWAUKEE, WI 53213

Visit Hal Leonard Online at
www.halleonard.com

Visit Phillip at
www.phillipkeveren.com

PREFACE

The best popular songs from every era eventually become "standards." These songs end up being arranged for myriad ensembles and "covered" by multiple artists in the popular, jazz, and even classical worlds. Most of selections in this collection are from the '70s, with a few from the '60s, '80s, and '90s added to the mix.

Using classical compositional devices, these enduring songs have been developed into character pieces for piano solo.

Musically yours,

Phillip Keveren

BIOGRAPHY

Phillip Keveren, a multi-talented keyboard artist and composer, has composed original works in a variety of genres from piano solo to symphonic orchestra. Mr. Keveren gives frequent concerts and workshops for teachers and their students in the United States, Canada, Europe, and Asia. Mr. Keveren holds a B.M. in composition from California State University Northridge and a M.M. in composition from the University of Southern California.

CONTENTS

ALL BY MYSELF

Music by SERGEI RACHMANINOFF
Words and Additional Music by
ERIC CARMEN
Arranged by Phillip Keveren

With melancholy ($\quarternote$ = 112)

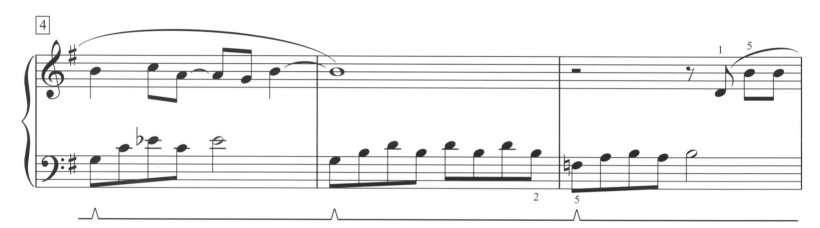

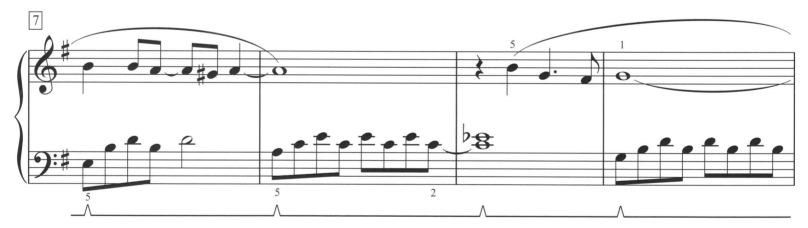

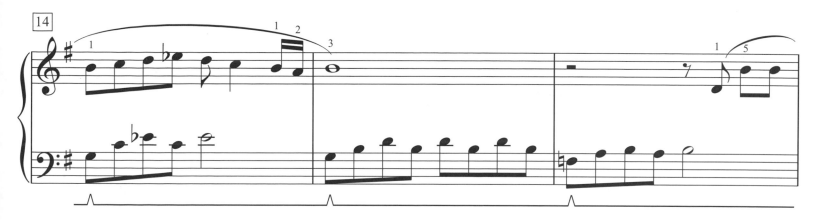

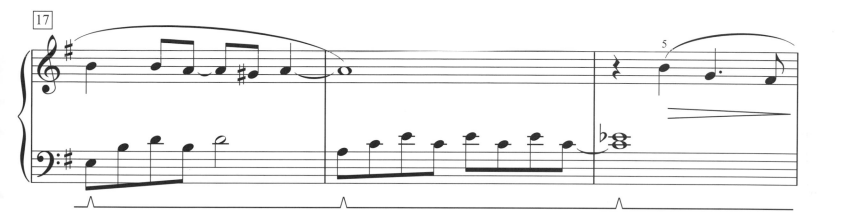

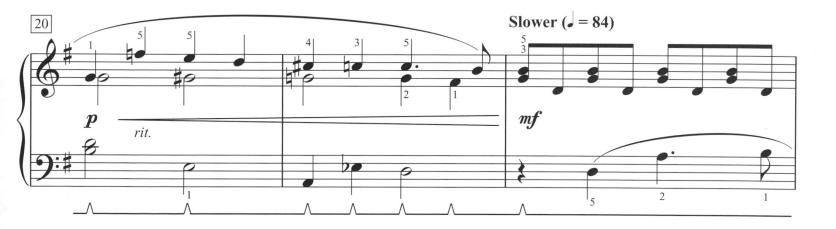

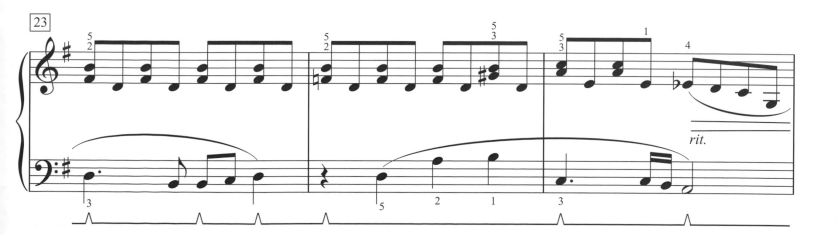

6

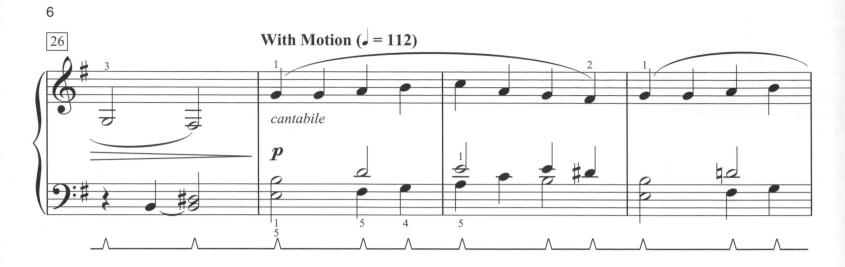

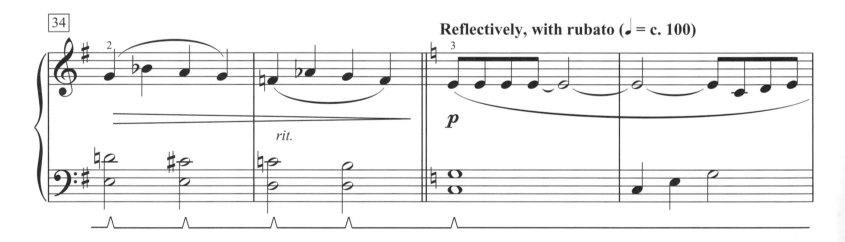

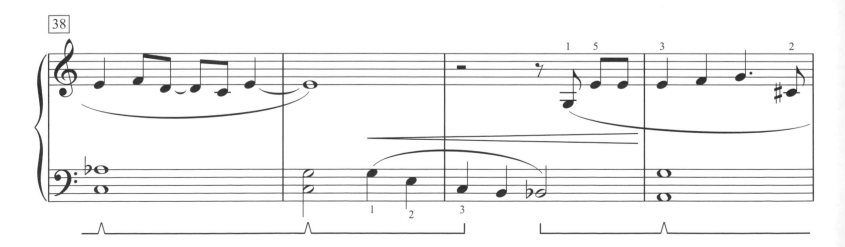

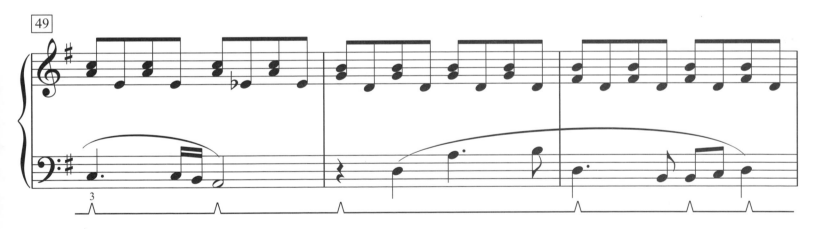

EVERY BREATH YOU TAKE

Music and Lyrics by
STING
Arranged by Phillip Keveren

With fluidity (♩ = 120)

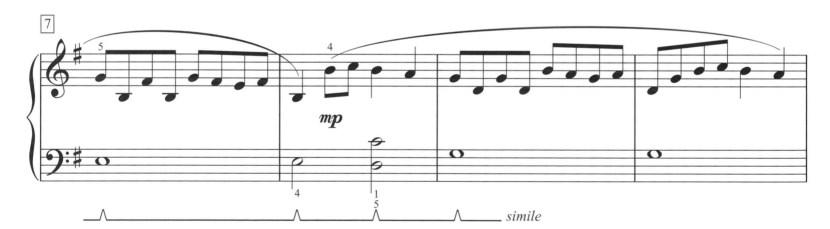

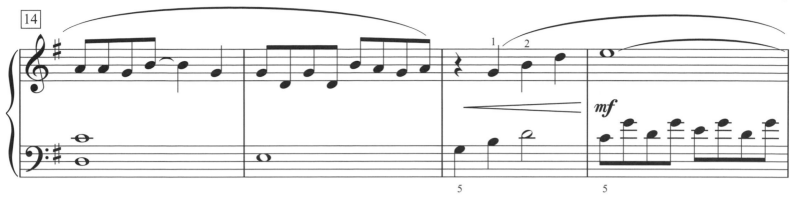

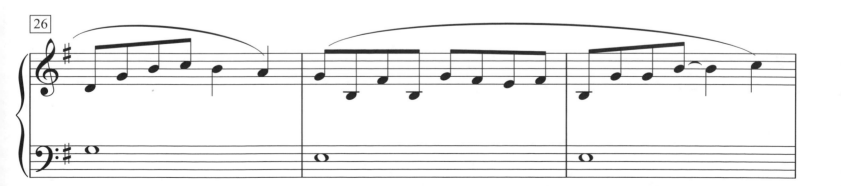

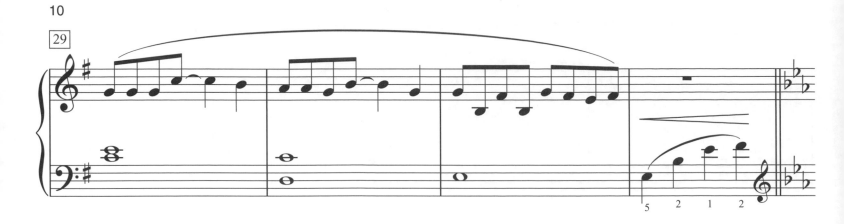

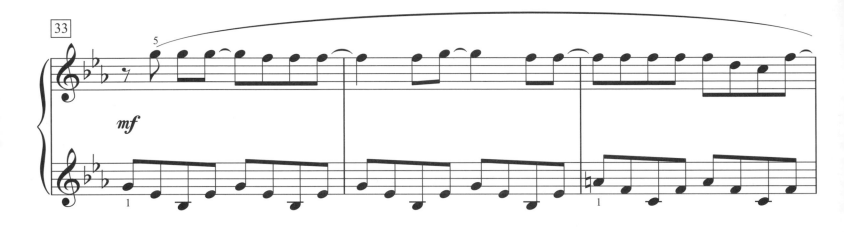

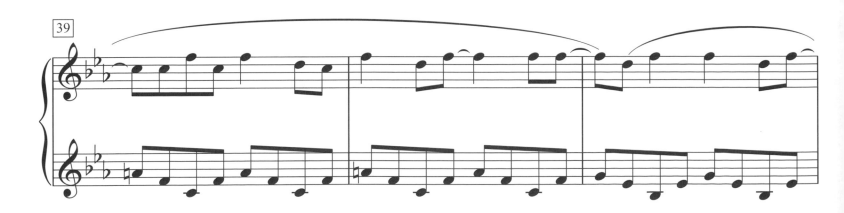

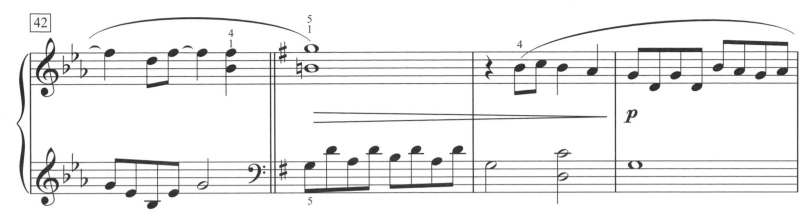

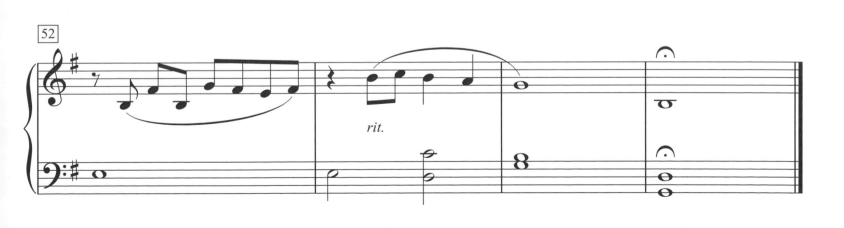

FIELDS OF GOLD

Music and Lyrics by
STING
Arranged by Phillip Keveren

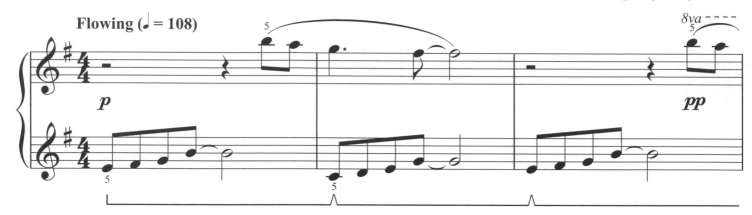

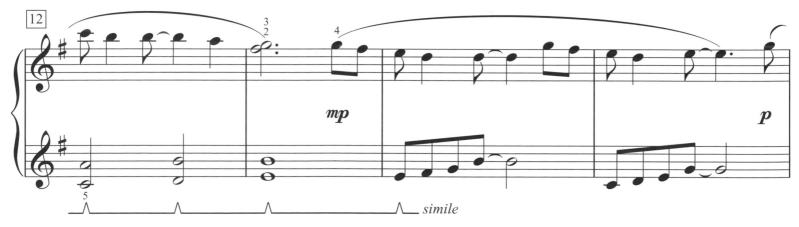

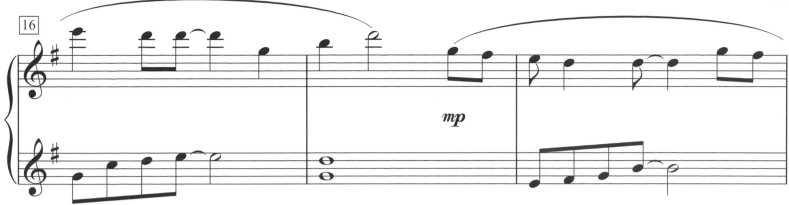

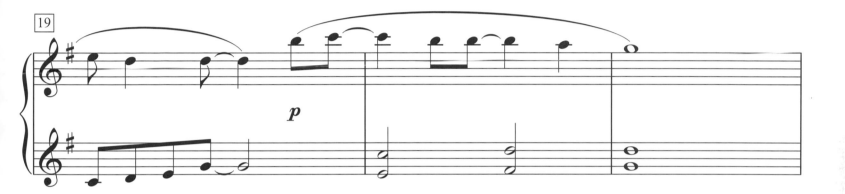

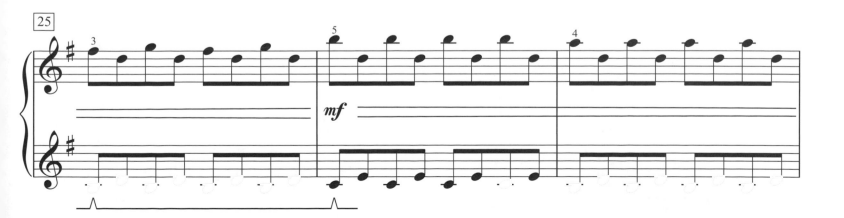

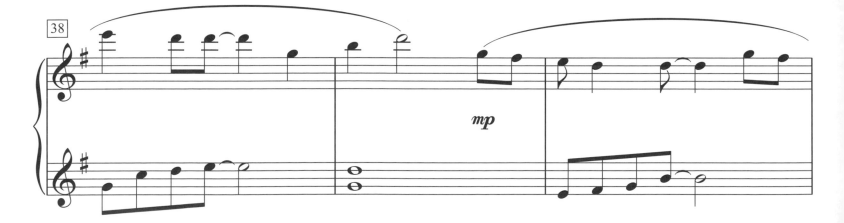

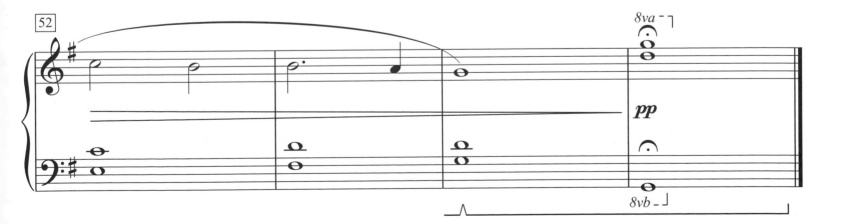

GOD ONLY KNOWS

Words and Music by BRIAN WILSON
and TONY ASHER
Arranged by Phillip Keveren

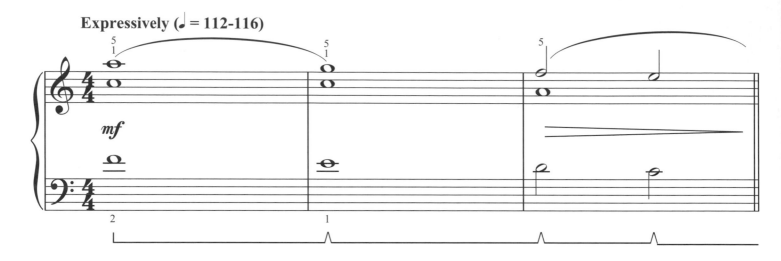

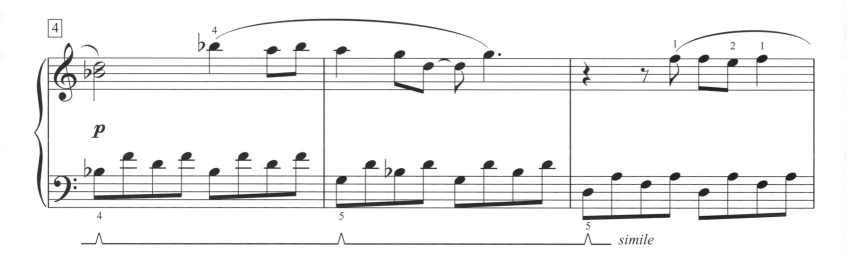

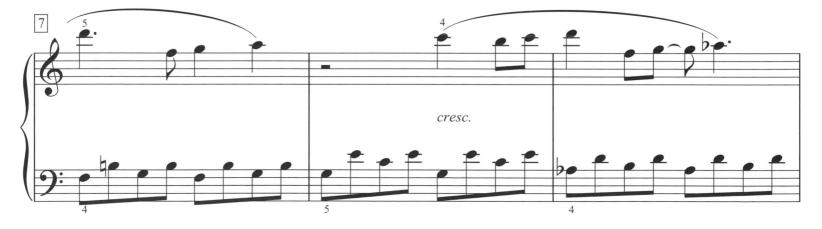

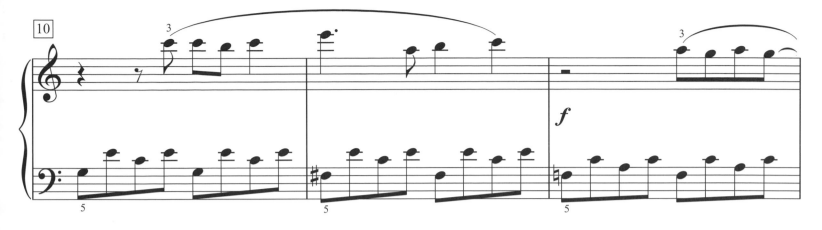

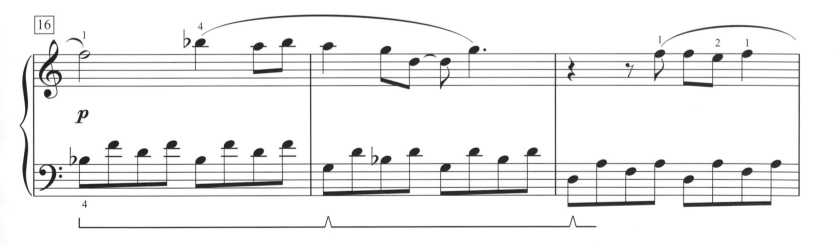

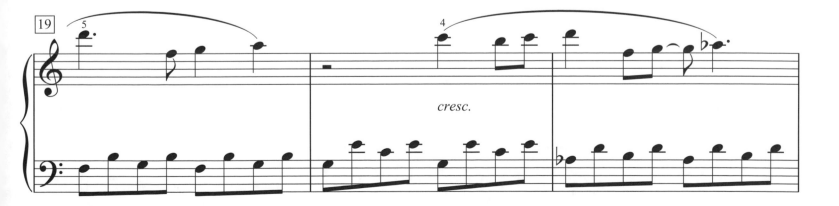

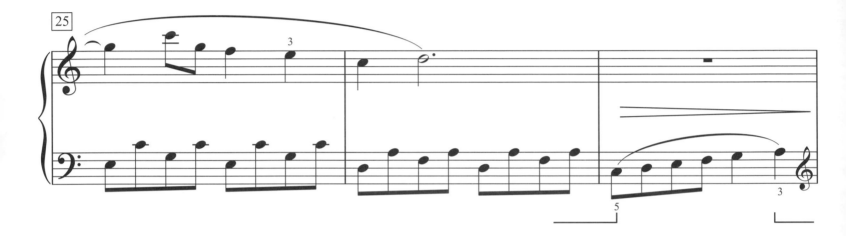

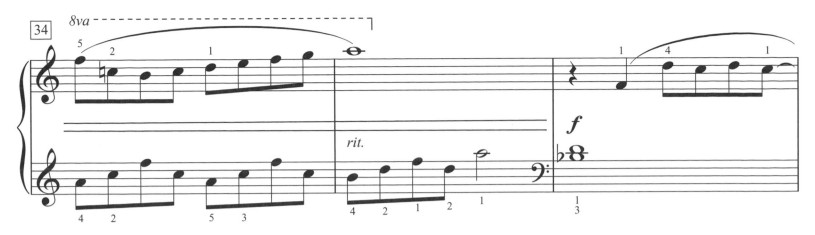

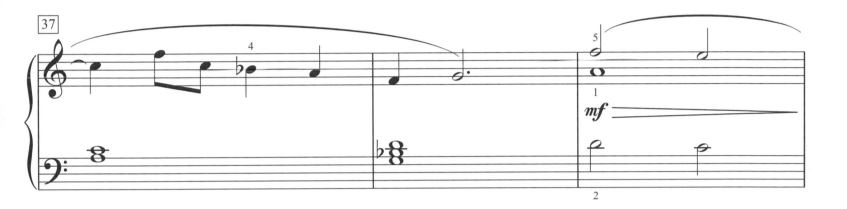

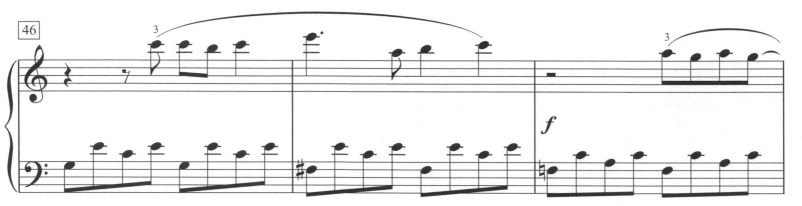

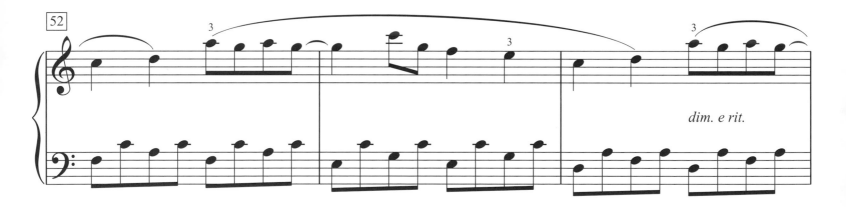

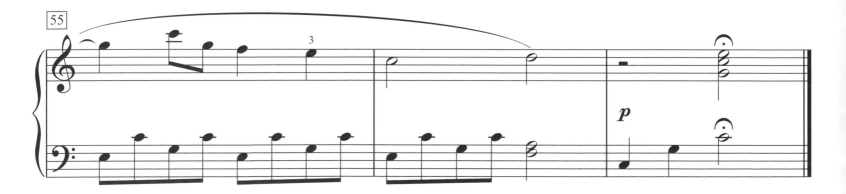

HOW DEEP IS YOUR LOVE

from the Motion Picture SATURDAY NIGHT FEVER

Words and Music by BARRY GIBB,
ROBIN GIBB and MAURICE GIBB
Arranged by Phillip Keveren

Dream-like (♩ = 88-92)

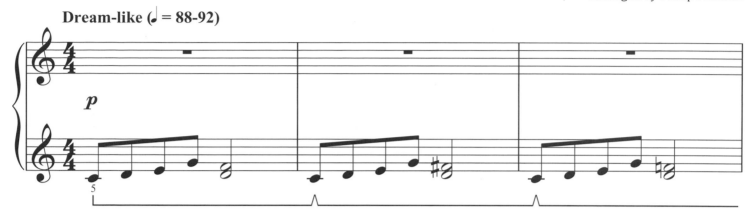

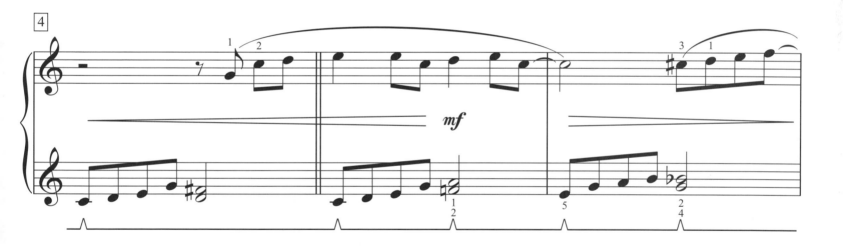

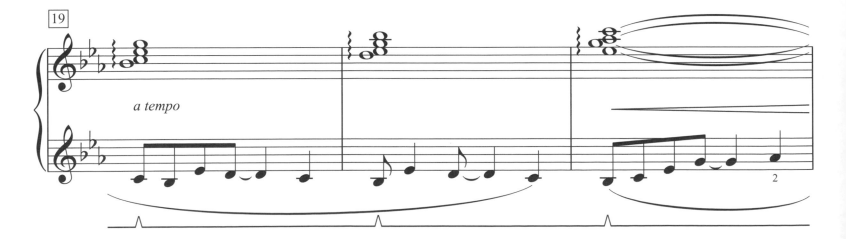

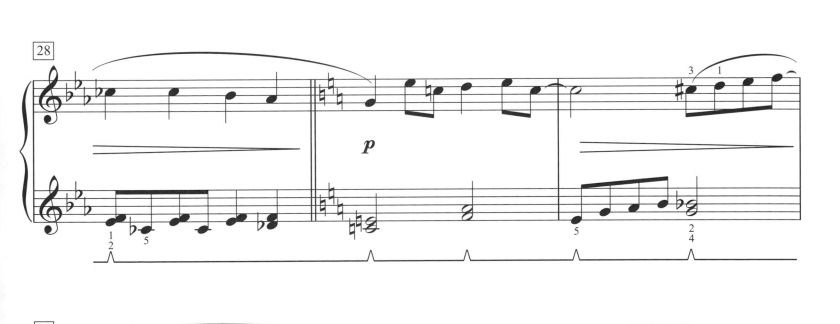

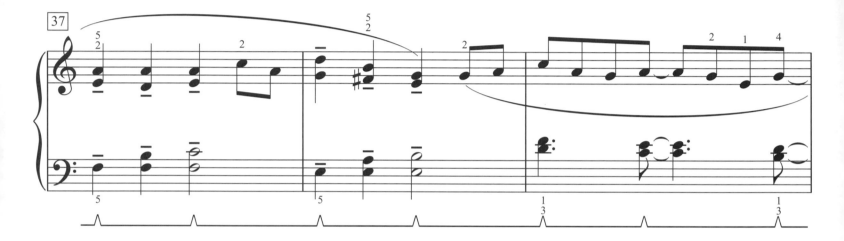

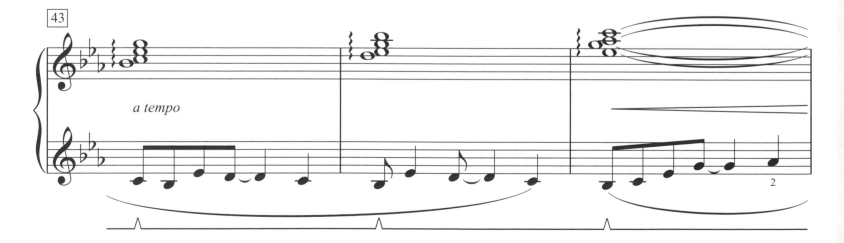

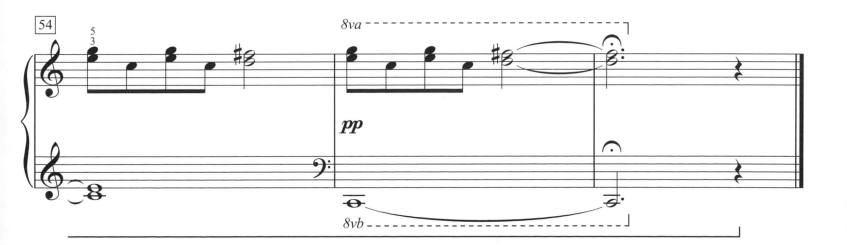

IF YOU LEAVE ME NOW

Words and Music by
PETER CETERA
Arranged by Phillip Keveren

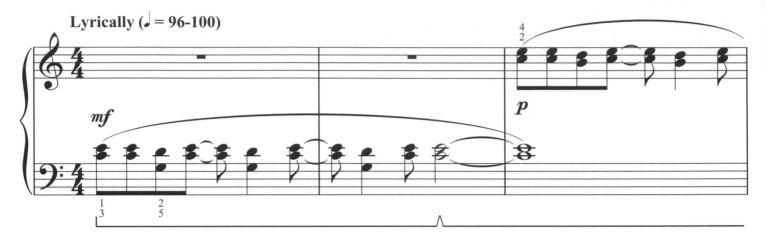

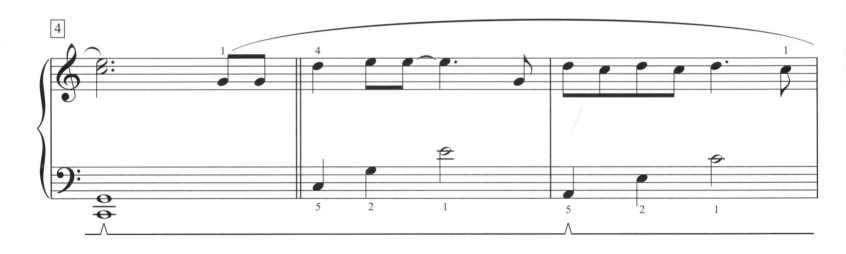

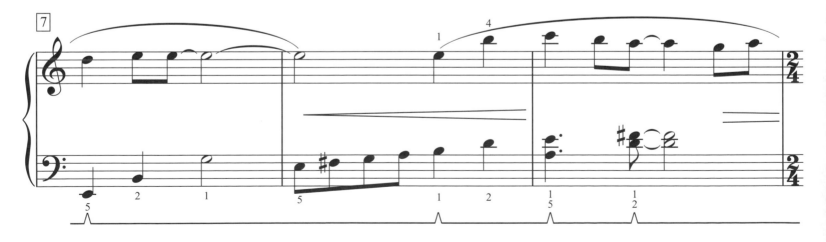

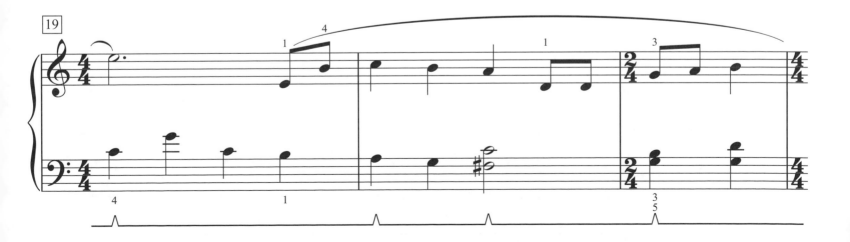

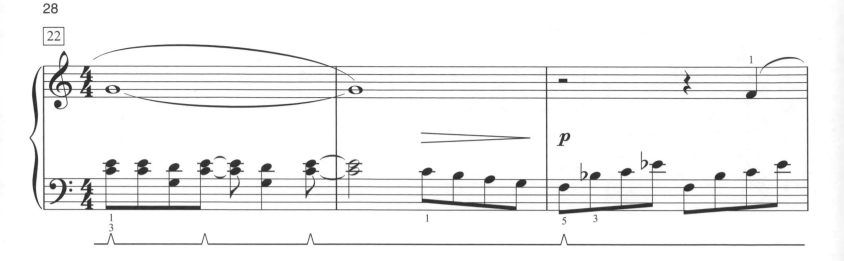

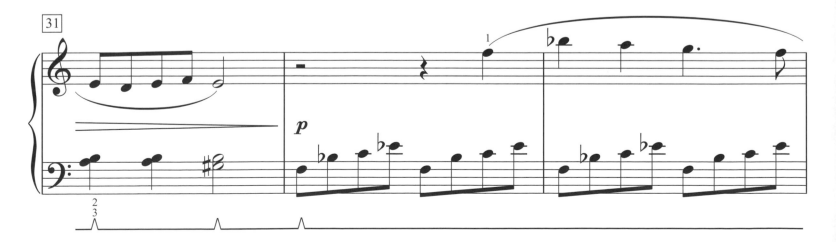

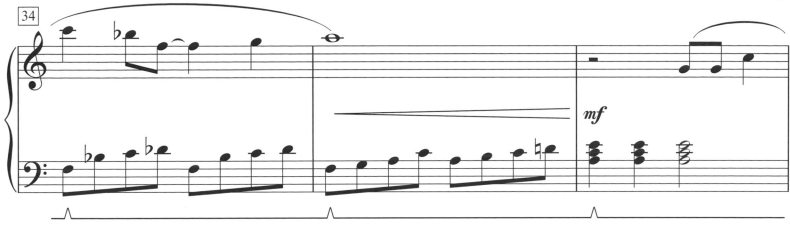

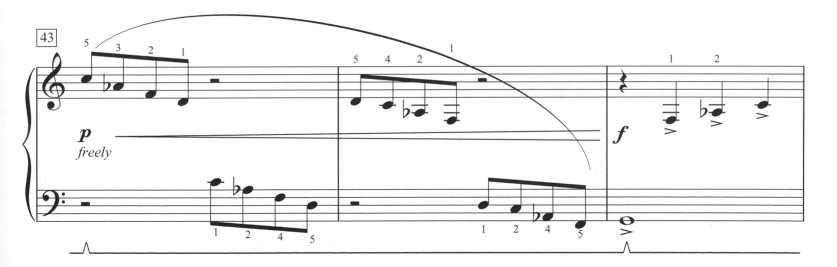

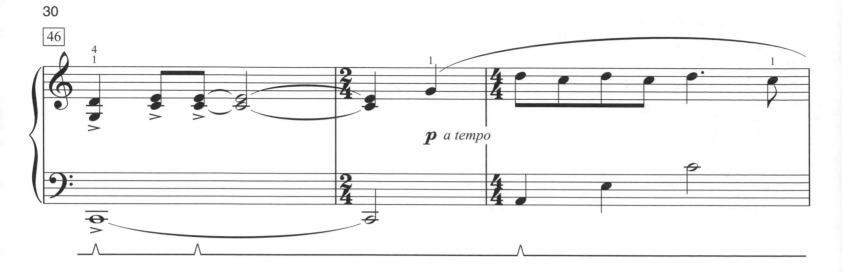

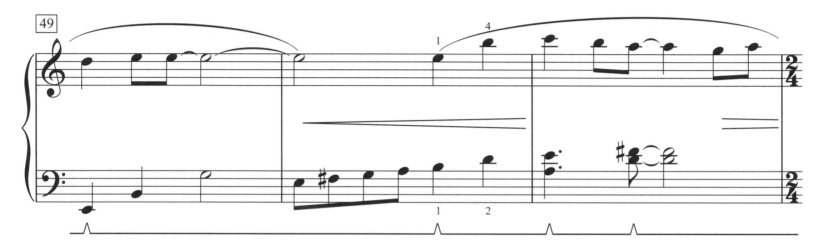

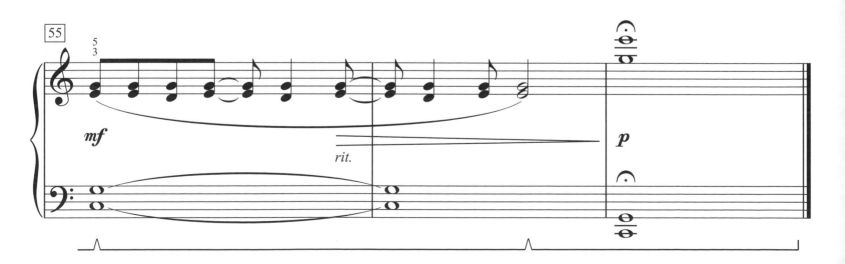

IT'S TOO LATE

Words and Music by CAROLE KING
and TONY STERN
Arranged by Phillip Keveren

With intensity (♩ = 120-126)

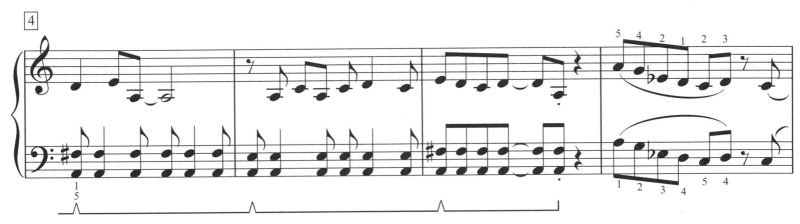

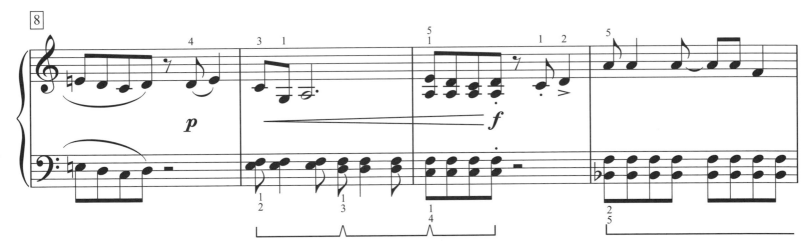

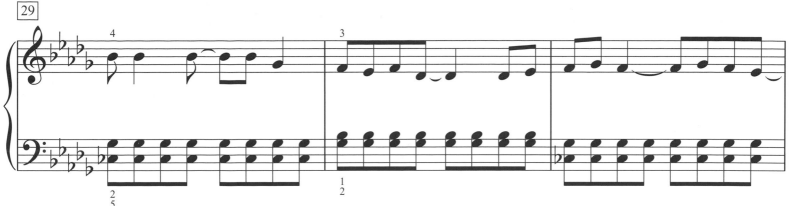

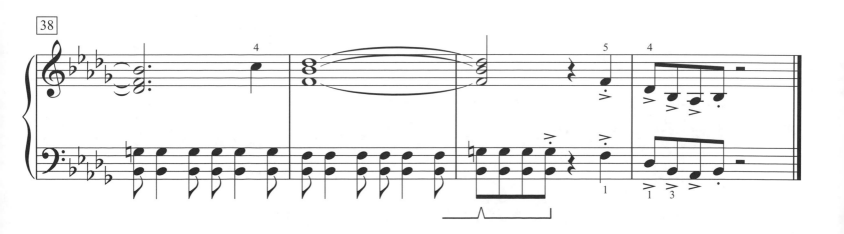

KILLING ME SOFTLY WITH HIS SONG

Words by NORMAN GIMBEL
Music by CHARLES FOX
Arranged by Phillip Keveren

Gently (♩ = 104)

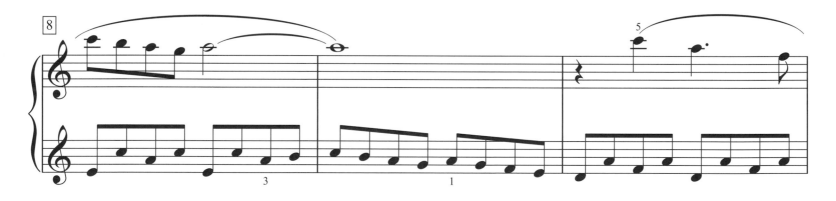

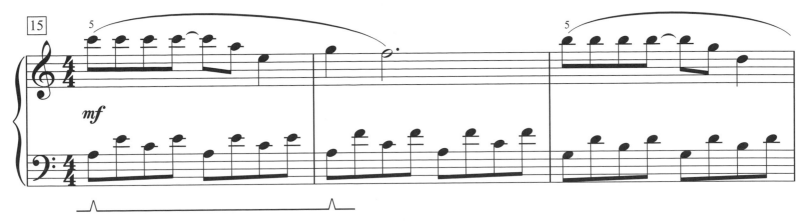

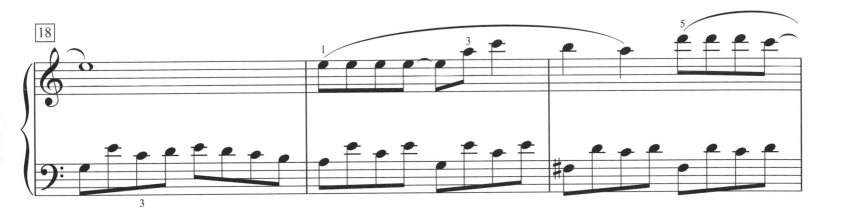

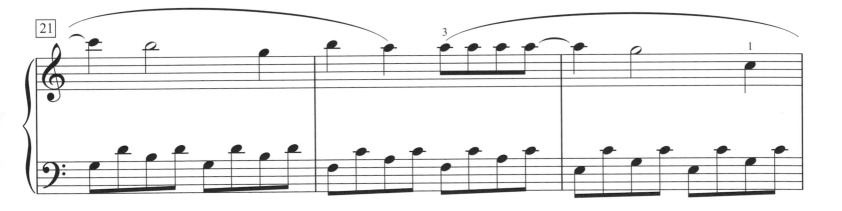

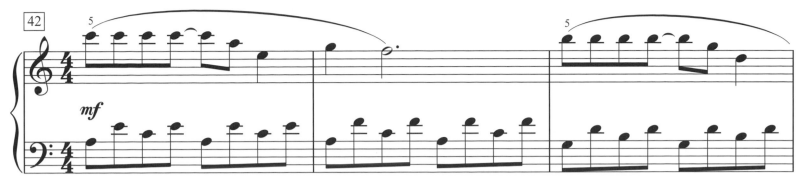

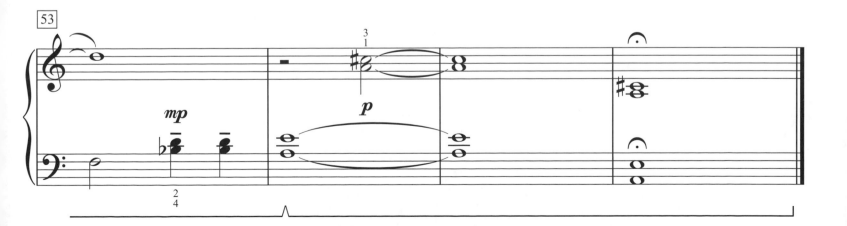

MAN IN THE MIRROR

Words and Music by GLEN BALLARD
and SIEDAH GARRETT
Arranged by Phillip Keveren

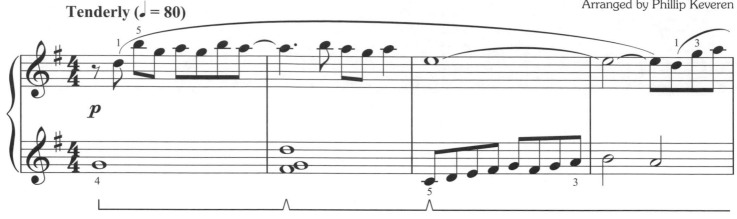

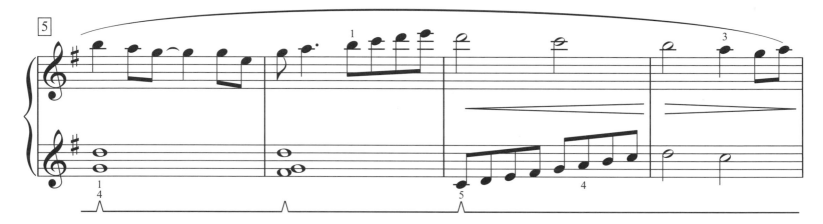

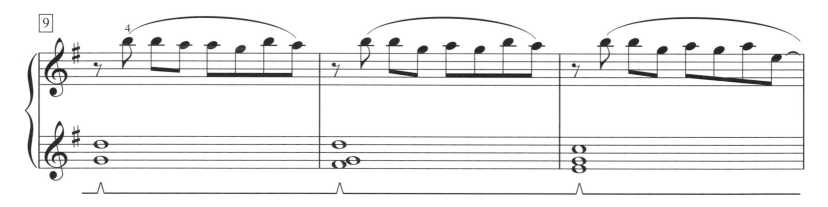

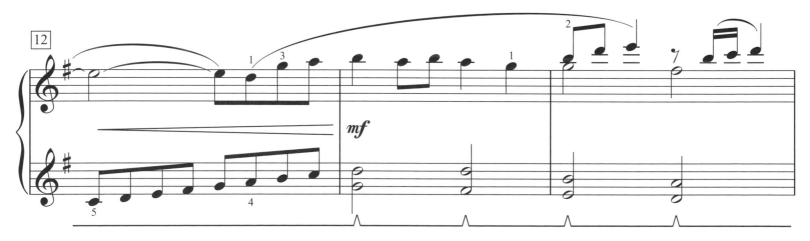

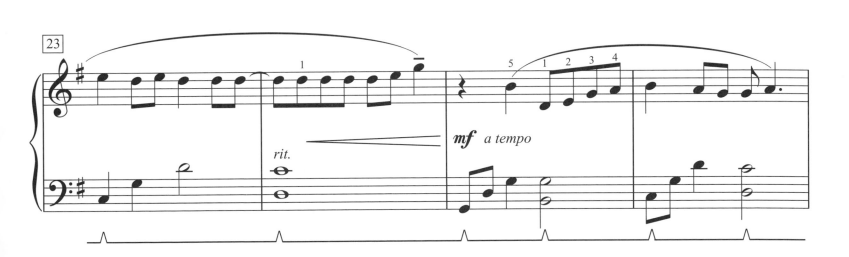

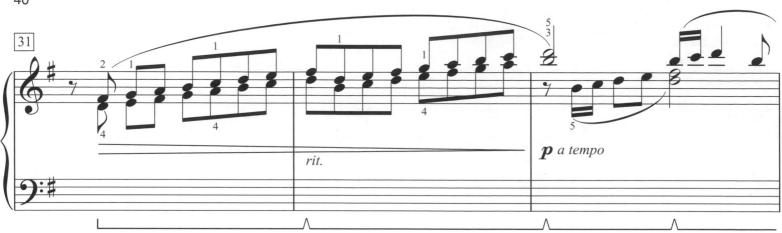

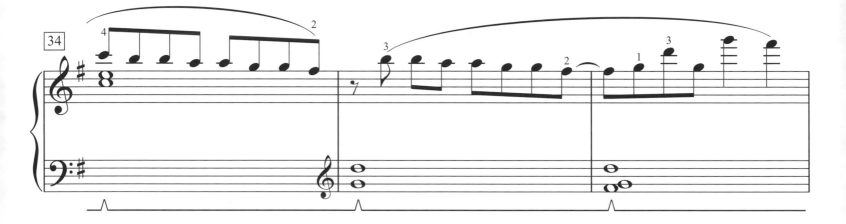

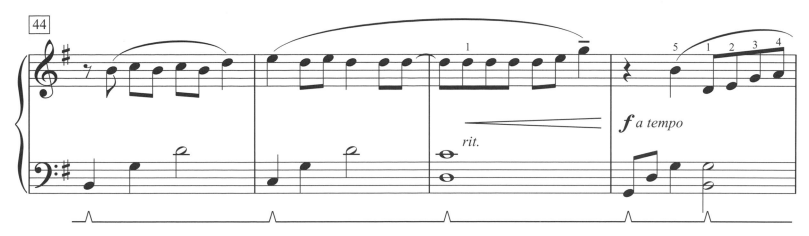

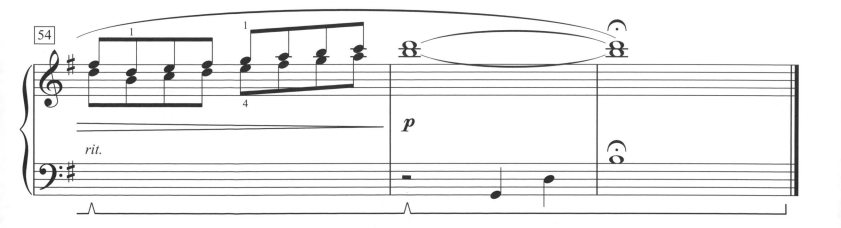

RAINY DAYS AND MONDAYS

Lyrics by PAUL WILLIAMS
Music by ROGER NICHOLS
Arranged by Phillip Keveren

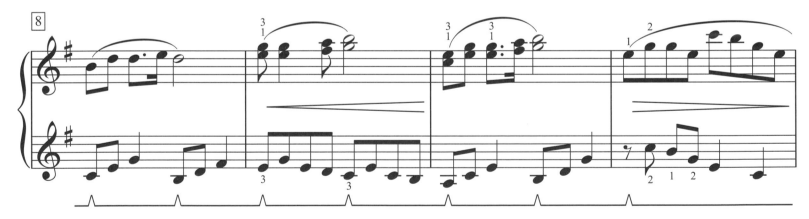

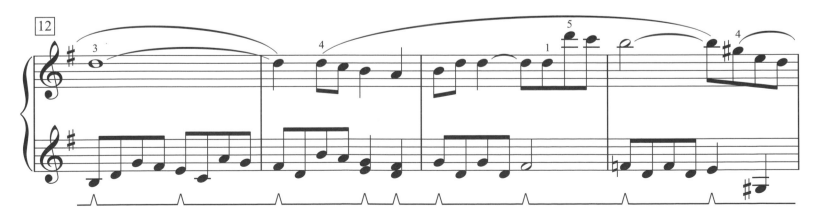

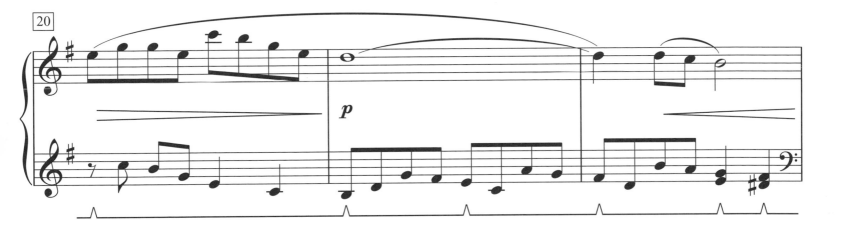

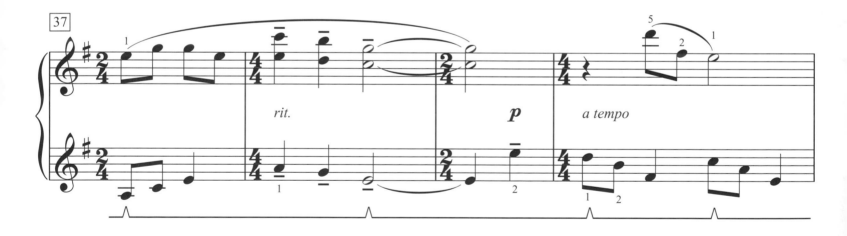

YOU ARE SO BEAUTIFUL

Words and Music by BILLY PRESTON
and BRUCE FISHER
Arranged by Phillip Keveren

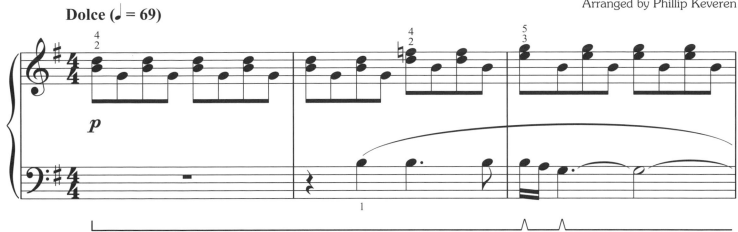

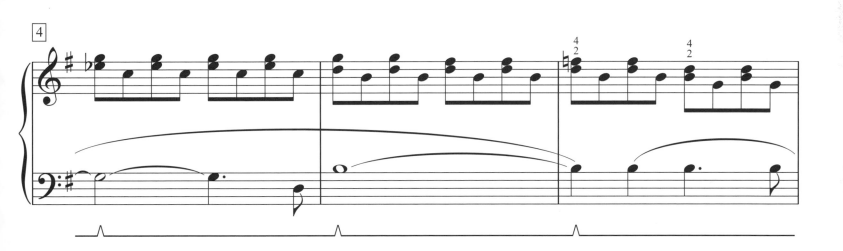

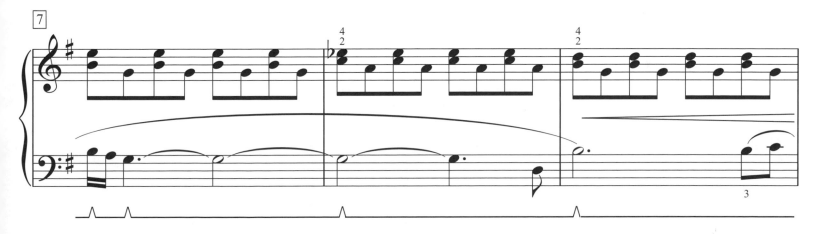

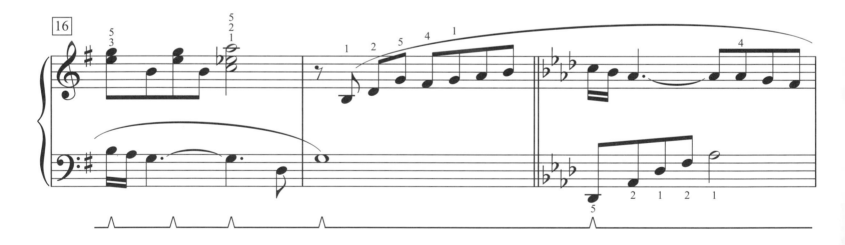

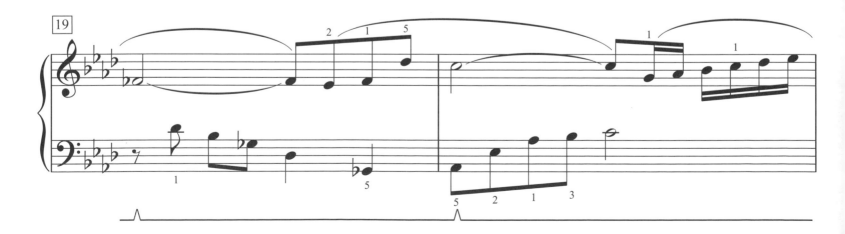

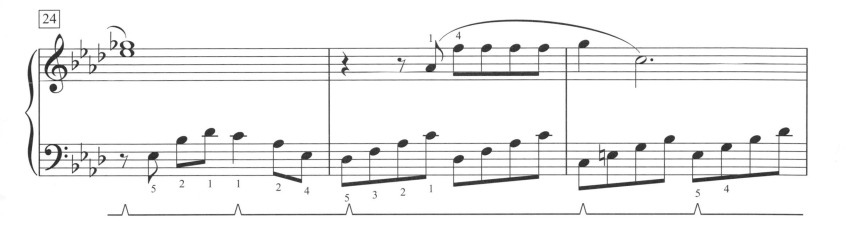

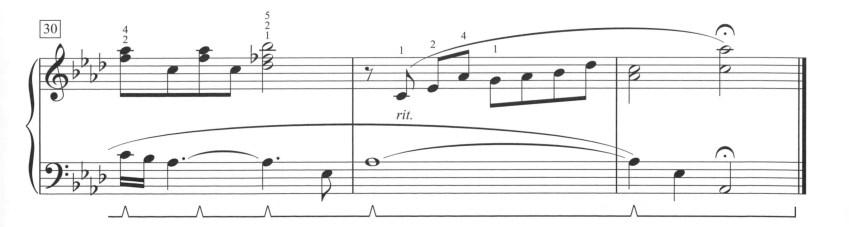

TIME AFTER TIME

Words and Music by CYNDI LAUPER
and ROB HYMAN
Arranged by Phillip Keveren

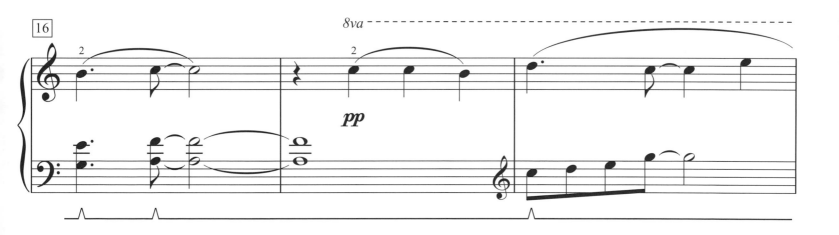

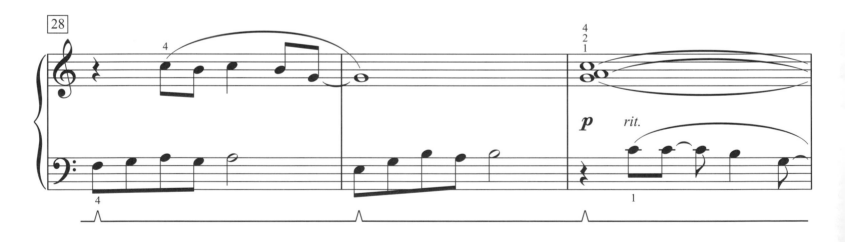

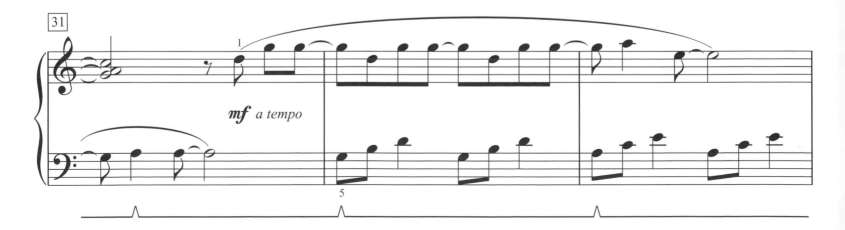

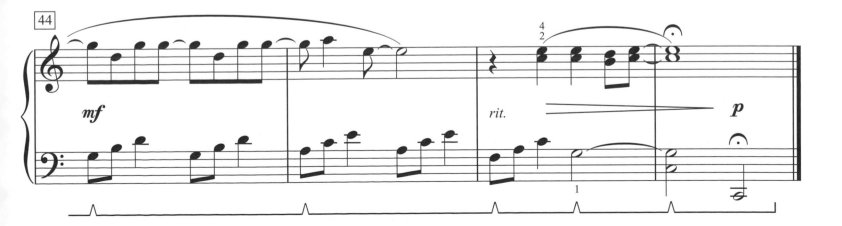

WALK ON BY

Lyric by HAL DAVID
Music by BURT BACHARACH
Arranged by Phillip Keveren

Flowing (♩ = 116)

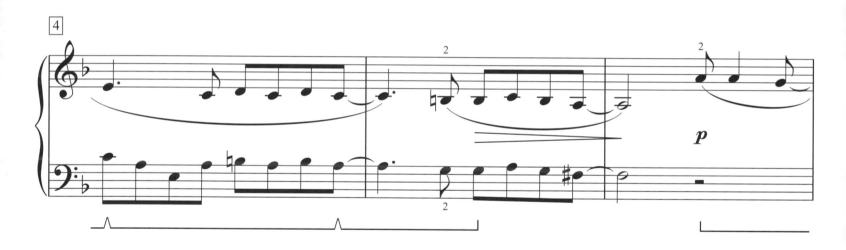

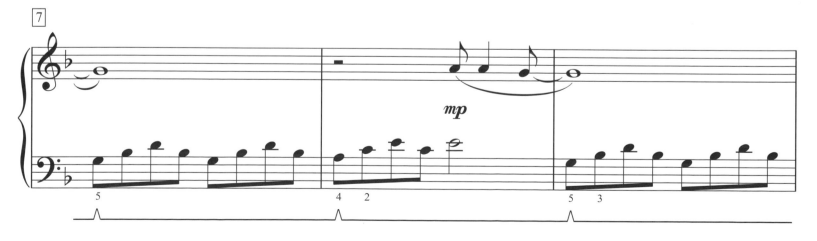

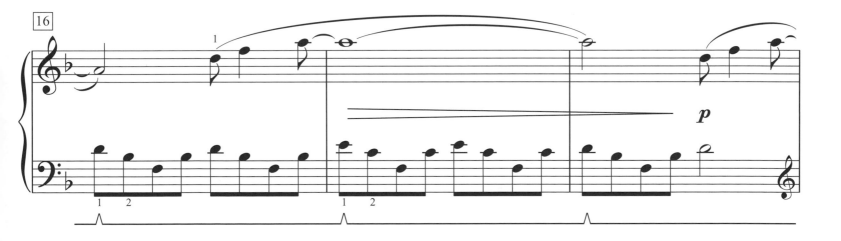

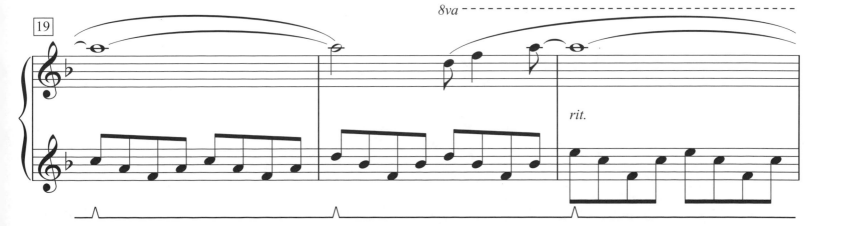

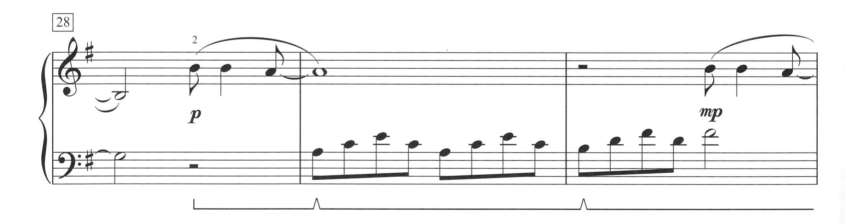

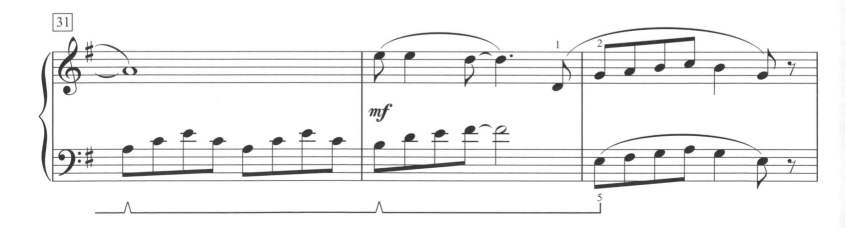

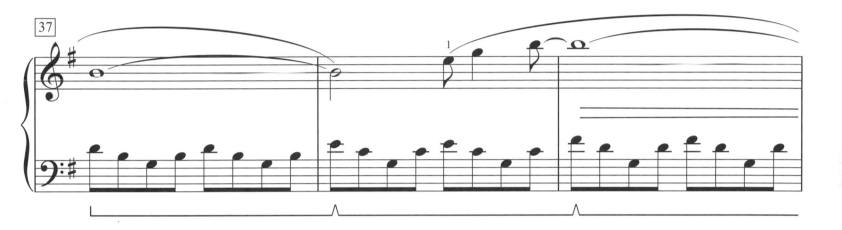

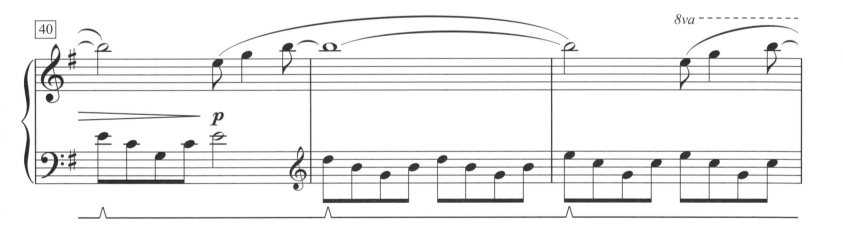

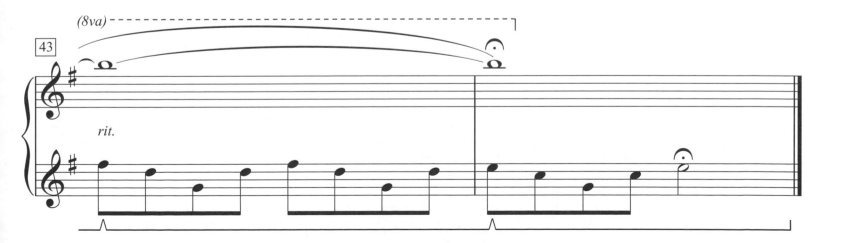

WE'VE ONLY JUST BEGUN

Words and Music by ROGER NICHOLS
and PAUL WILLIAMS
Arranged by Phillip Keveren

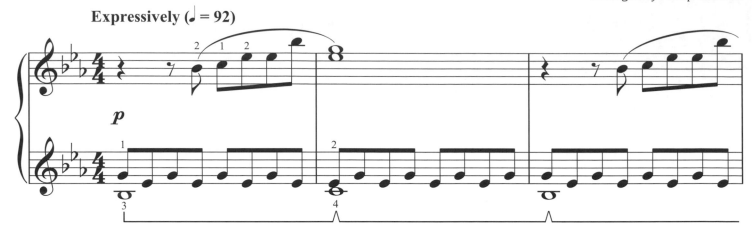

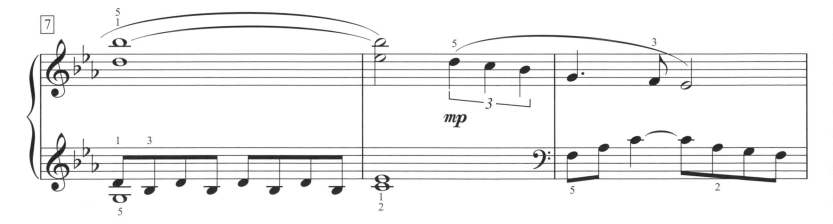

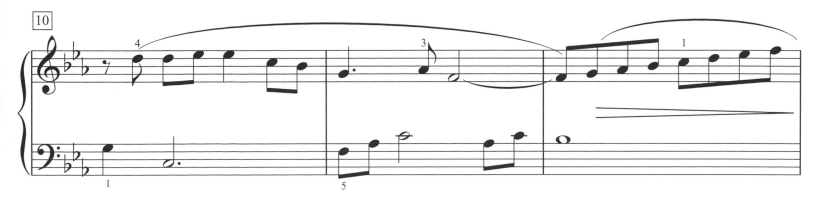

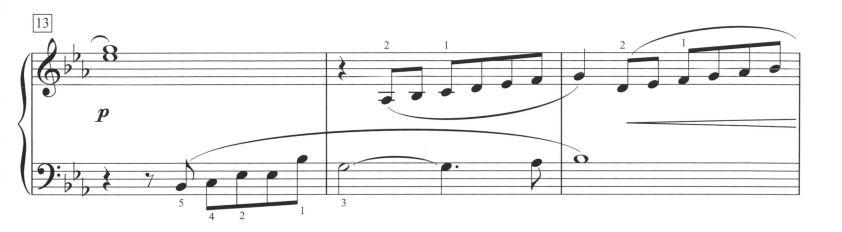

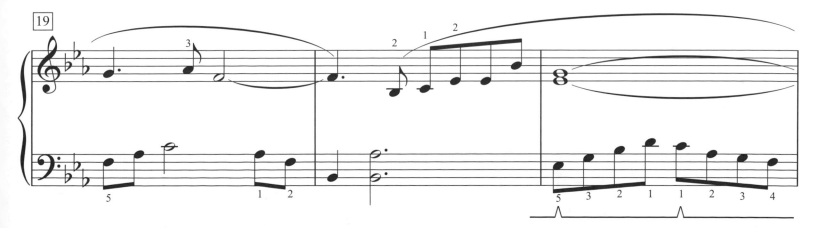

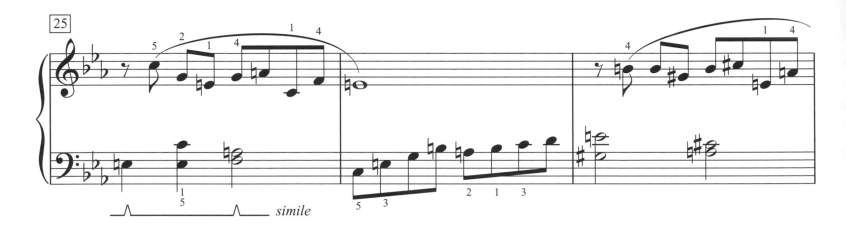

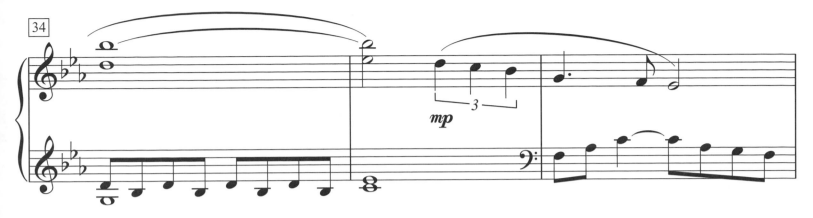

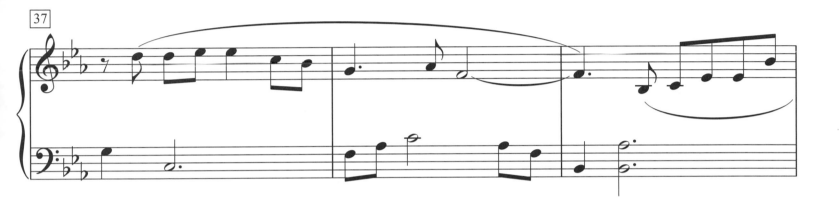

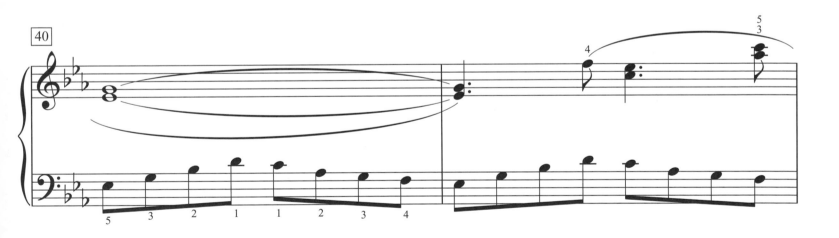

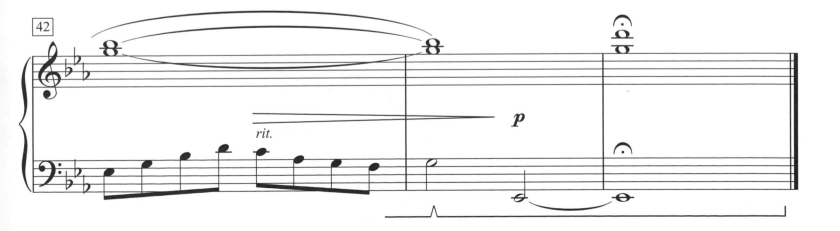

YOU'VE GOT A FRIEND

Words and Music by
CAROLE KING
Arranged by Phillip Keveren

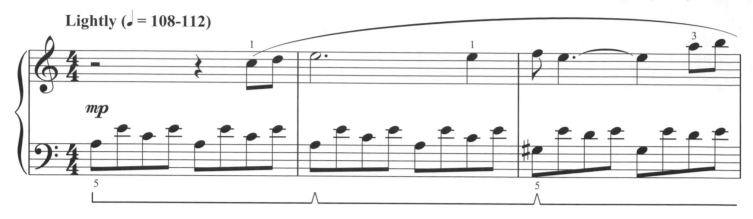

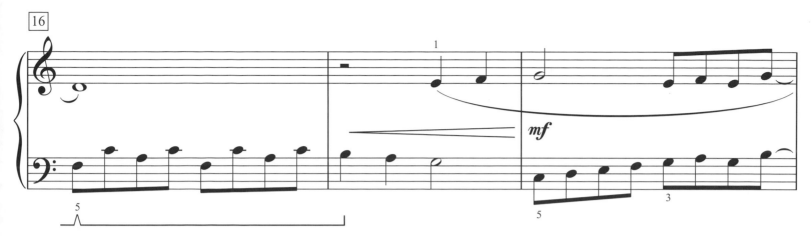

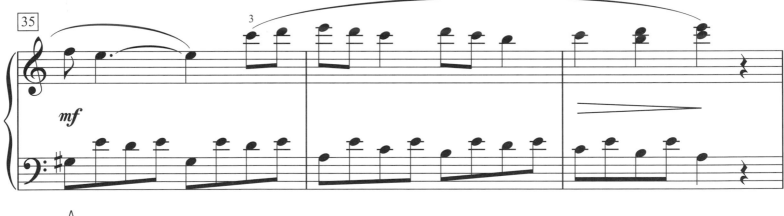

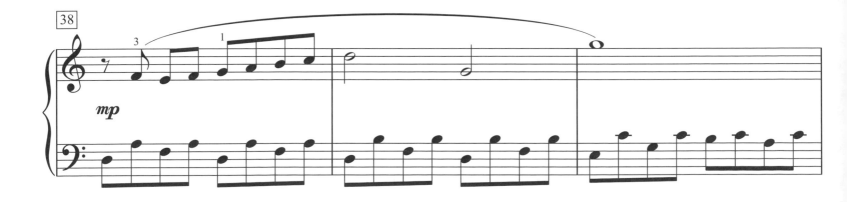

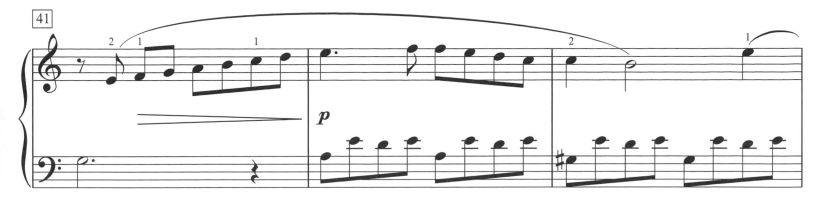

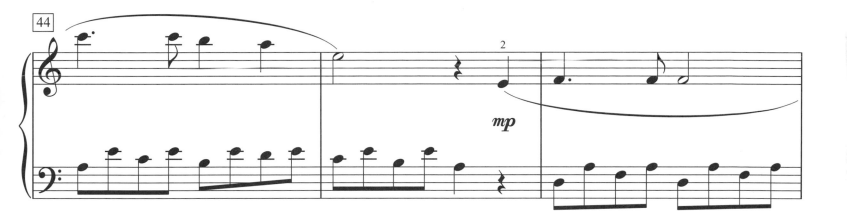

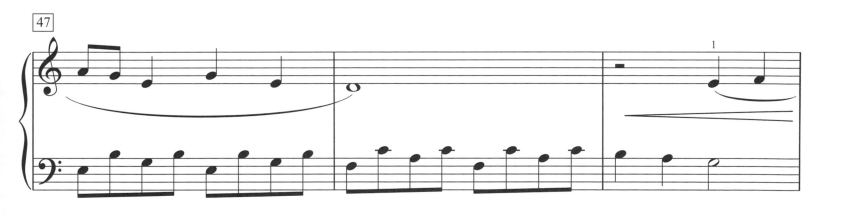

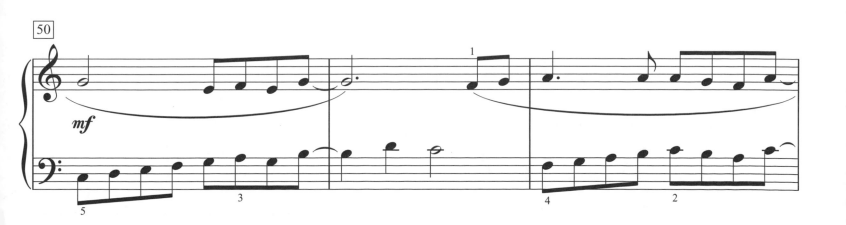

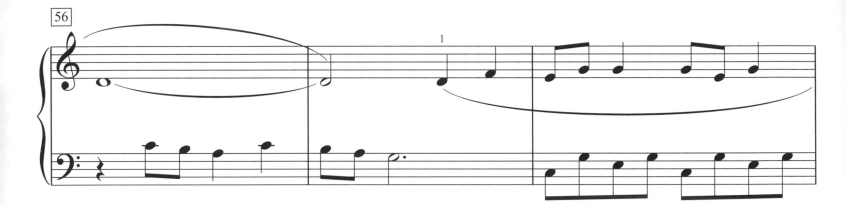

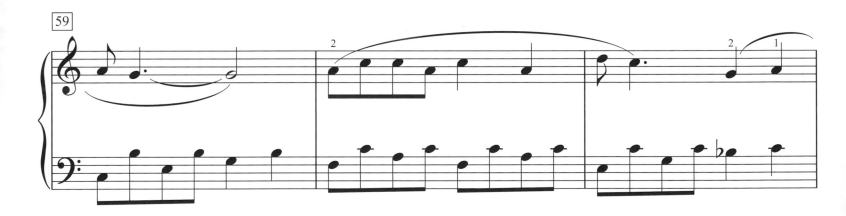

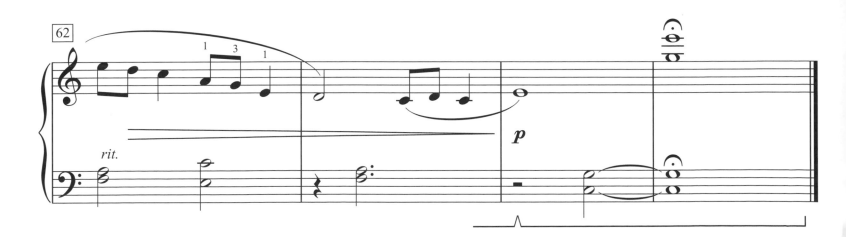